# Yog the Hog

Written by Stephanie Bunt
Illustrated by Taylor Gallion

"Yog the Hog" not only focuses on the short vowel O sound, but also teaches children that in life there may be things or places that they love. However, even if those things or places are no longer there, they can always find something or some place else that they will love just as much.

To Uncle Bill, thank you for showing me the importance of creating and following dreams in life. Imagination is the itch that can never be fully scratched! I love you.
- Stephanie

Thank you to my family and friends back home who encouraged me to chase my dreams.
-Taylor

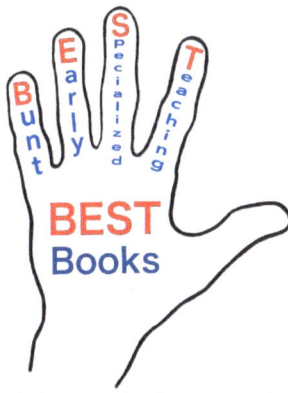

Short "o" Vowel Sound Practice

This book was created using the B.E.S.T. method.

Before reading this book with your early reader, practice reading these words. First, read them to your early reader while pointing to the sounds each word makes. Then, have your early reader try. Point to each sound as he/she is reading the words and say the sounds to him/her, as needed. Begin reading the story once your early reader feels comfortable with these words.

When reading the story, read to your early reader a few times. As you are reading, point to the sounds/words you are reading. Now, have your early reader read. Point to the sounds/words as he/she is reading and say the sounds with him/her, as needed. Happy reading!

You can cut out these focus words at the end of the book.

First, practice these words.

# Yog, dog, log, hog, fog, frog, bog, sob, sod, odd

Once these words are mastered, go onto the next set of words.

# on, hop, drop, stop, rot, not, hot, spot

Once these words are mastered, review the first set and go onto the next set of words.

# moss, rock, fond, pond, jolly

After practicing these words, review all the words.

Now, it's time to read the book, yay!

The definitions of some of these words are in the back of the book.
Explaining these words will help your child understand them.

Yog, the hog, is fond of his log.

# Yog's log is by the bog, on a pond.

A frog hops
by Yog's log
on the pond.

A frog is on moss in the fog, by the log, in the bog.

Now, Yog and Dog
are on the log
in the fog.

Yog and Dog are
fond of the spot
on the log,
on the pond.

Uh oh, the log
has rot!

# Yog and Dog drop in the pond.

# Yog and Dog sob.

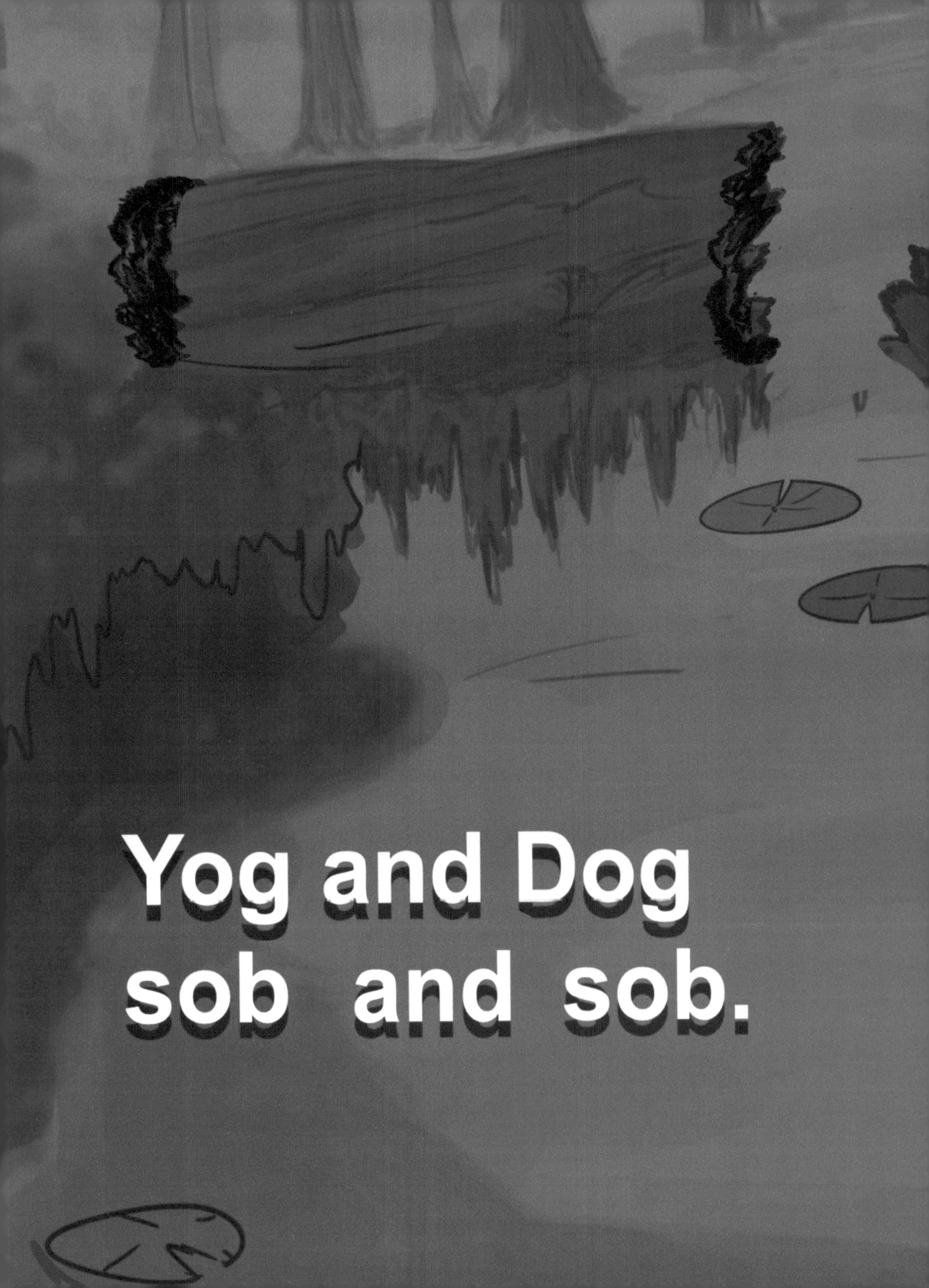

Yog and Dog
sob and sob.

Now, Yog and Dog are not fond of the log by the bog, on the pond.

Now, Yog and Dog are fond of the odd rock.

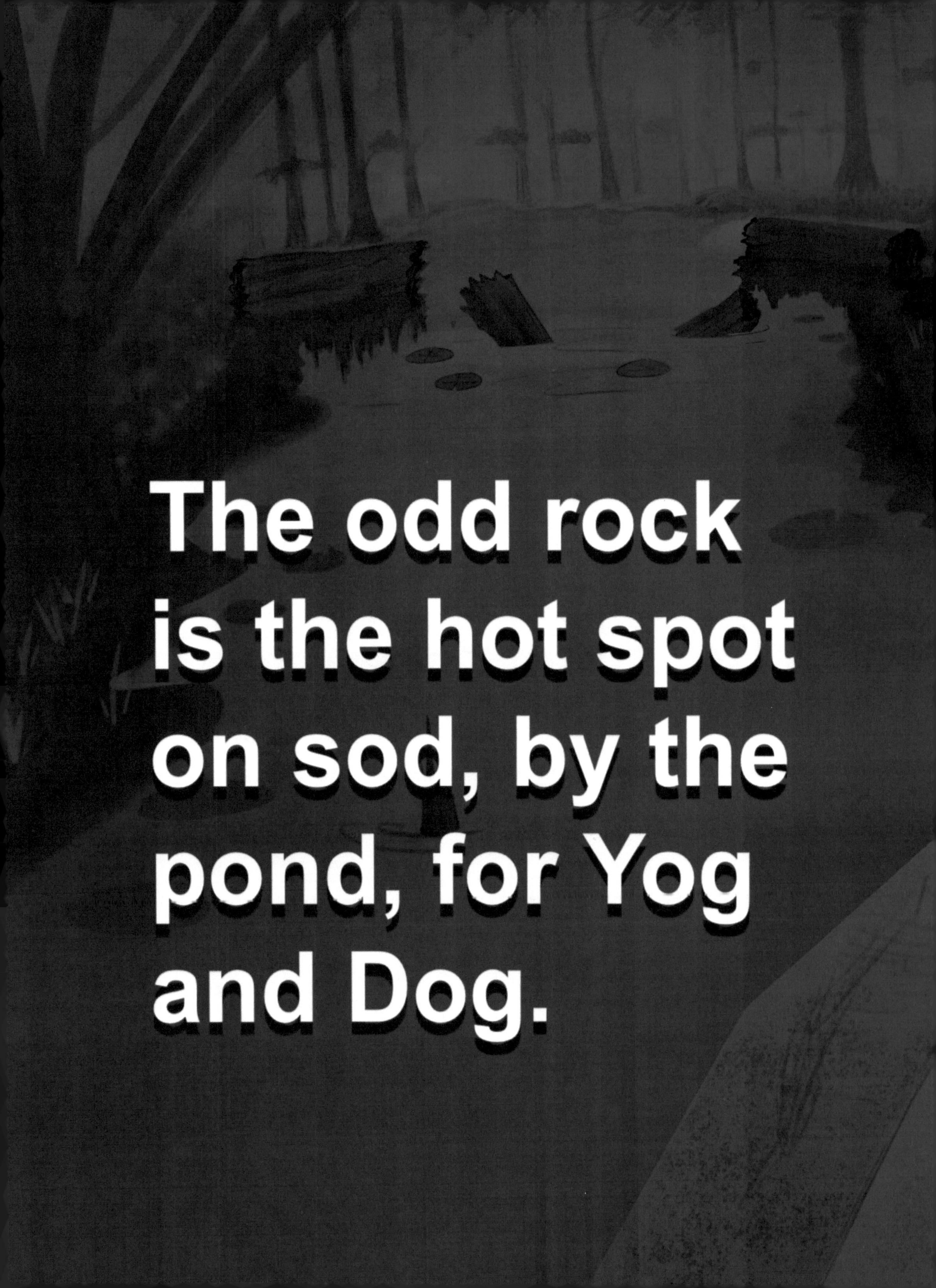

The odd rock is the hot spot on sod, by the pond, for Yog and Dog.

Jolly! Yog and Dog hop and hop on the rock, on the sod.

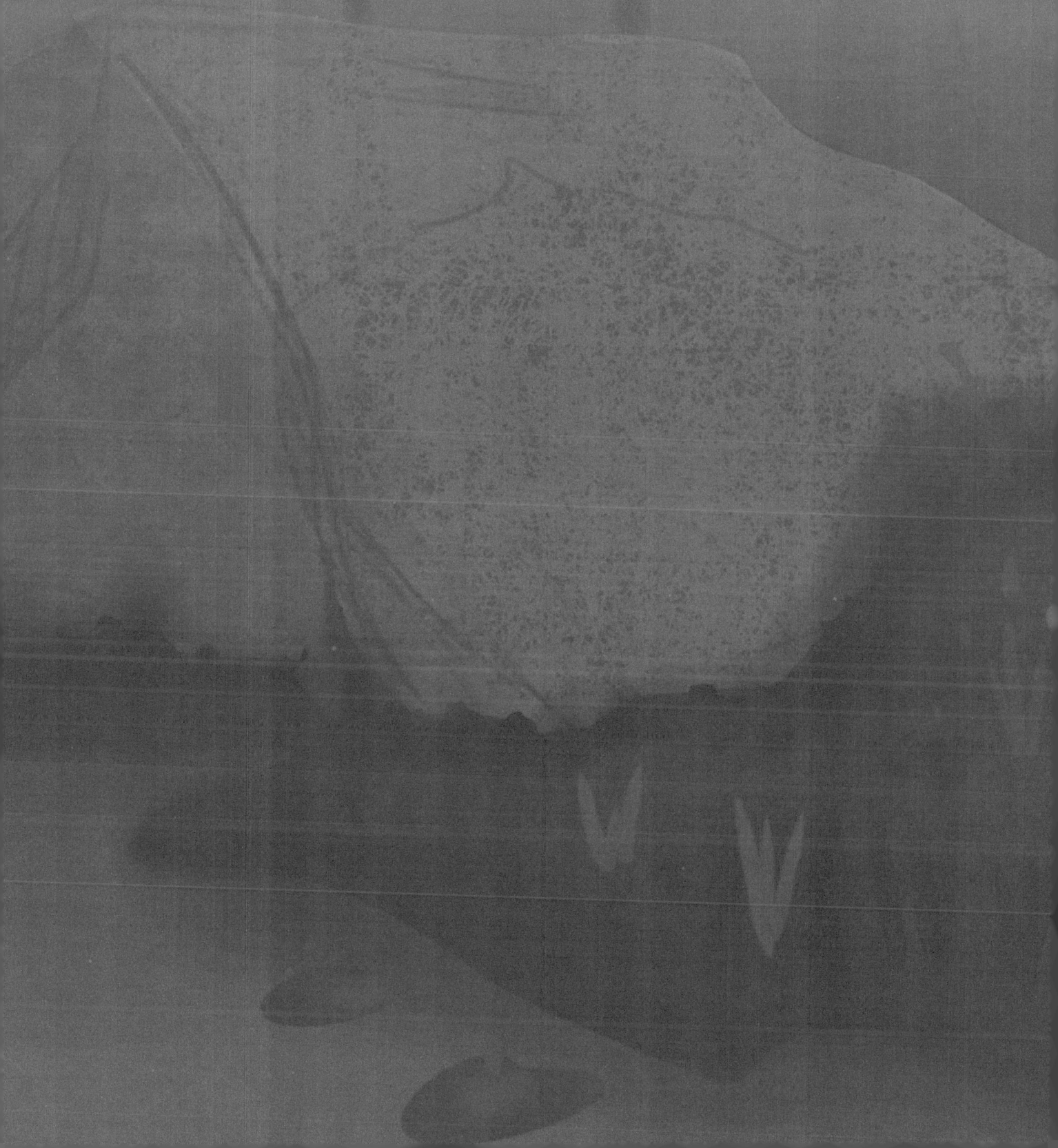

# About the Author

Stephanie Bunt has been working with special-needs children for more than 17 years. She loves writing, teaching children, and has done extensive research creating teaching strategies and curricula for children. She went to undergraduate and graduate school at the University of California, Los Angeles (UCLA) in Psychology with a minor in Applied Developmental Psychology and graduate school in one of the best Educational Psychology programs in the country at UCLA. She also works as an adjunct professor at Whittier College.

# About the Illustrator

Taylor Gallion is an artist from Wichita, Kansas, who moved out to Los Angeles to use his talent for drawing and made it his dream job! Growing up, Taylor was inspired by movies and cartoons. Taylor has his bachelor's degree in animation, and is constantly working with new people bringing their ideas to life.

# BEST
## Books

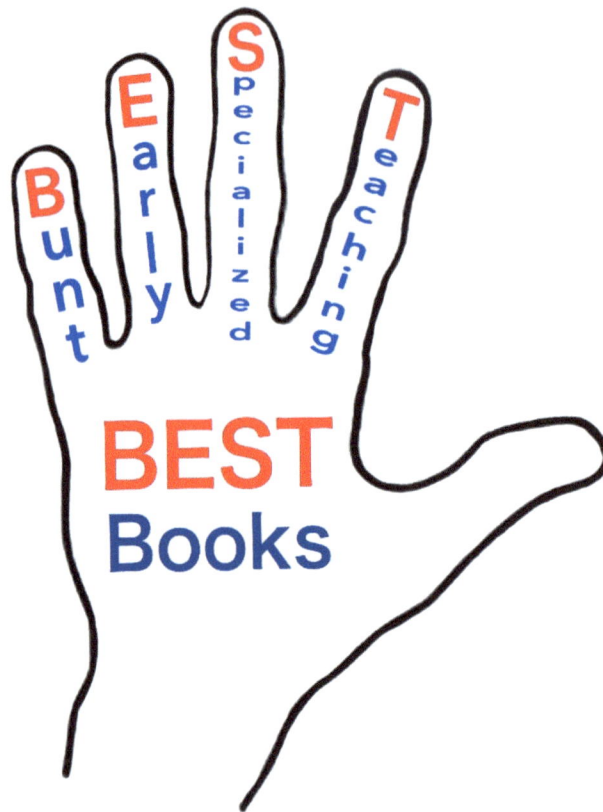

**B**unt
**E**arly
**S**pecialized
**T**eaching

# Bunt Early Specialized Teaching

# Definitions

**Explain these words to your child for a better understanding of the book.**

Bog: Wet or muddy ground too soft to support a heavy body

Fond: Loving, adoring, or liking

Odd: Different from what is usual

Rot: To become weak from decay or be ruined

Sob: To cry

Sod: Solid ground or grass

For extra practice cut out these words and read them.

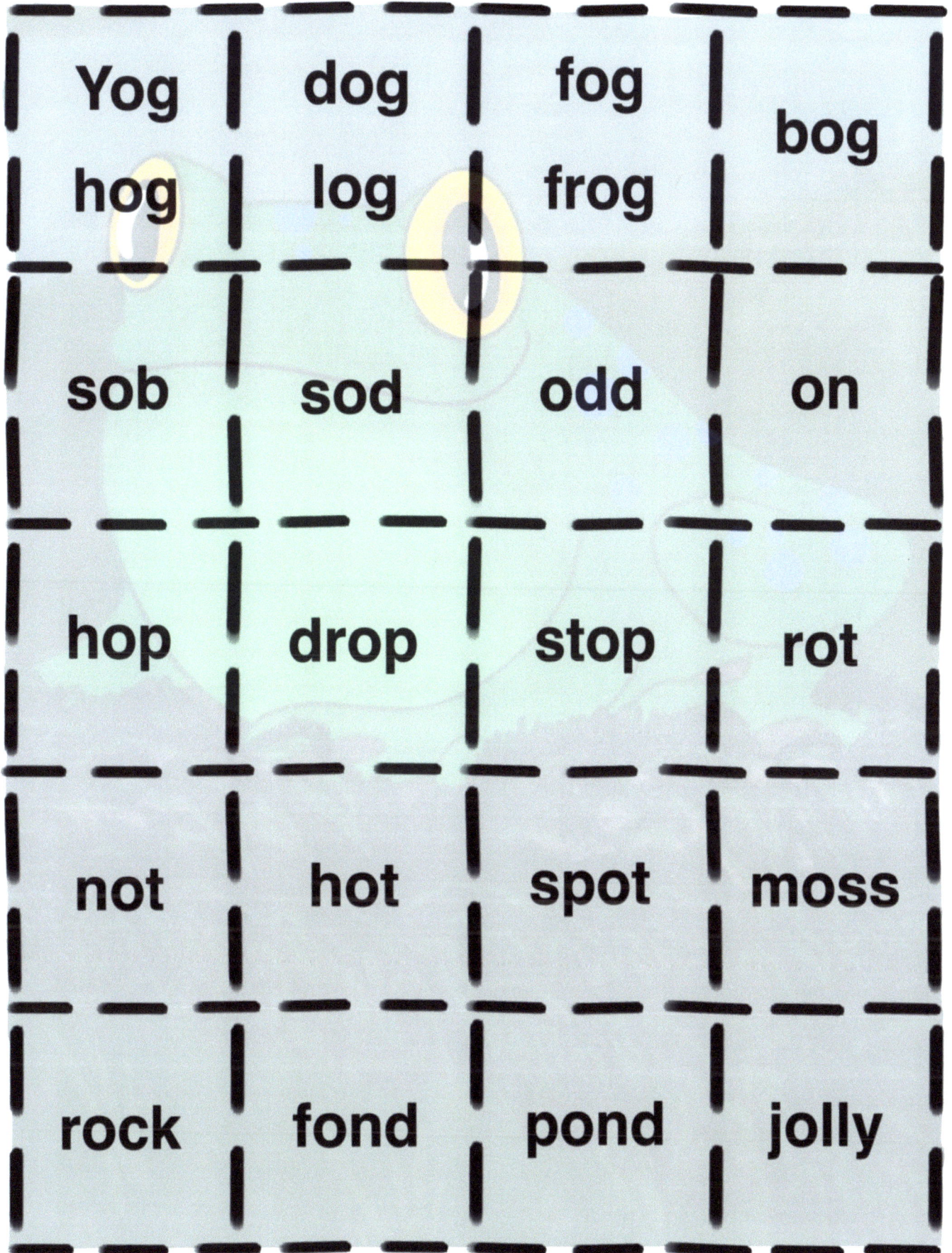

| Yog | dog | fog | |
|-----|-----|------|------|
| hog | log | frog | bog |
| sob | sod | odd | on |
| hop | drop | stop | rot |
| not | hot | spot | moss |
| rock | fond | pond | jolly |

For fun, you can also put these pieces back together to make a puzzle.

**Copyright, 2018**